WARNING:

The book you are about to read (or better yet, purchase) is full of unfair, inaccurate, and vicious stereotypes and generalizations. There are no real individuals, living or dead, who correspond with any characterization included herein. So, if you come across something that makes you angry with the author for writing about you, just remember that you are WRONG, WRONG, WRONG!

Almost the Truth™ About Youth Ministry:

Salesmen, Secretaries, and Smart Alecks

Dewey Roth

Almost the Truth™ Publishing

Rosemount, Minnesota

A tiny division of SandTree Productions

Markle, Indiana

ALMOST THE TRUTH™ ABOUT YOUTH MINISTRY: Salesmen, Secretaries, and Smart Alecks
Copyright 2008 by Dewey Roth

Almost the Truth™ Publishing
16715 Gannon Ave W, Rosemount, Minnesota 55068

ISBN: 978-0-6151-8523-1

To my *Beloved*

God bless you for sticking with me through all the experiences that made this book "based on a true story."

And *Rick*

Most of this is your fault

CONTENTS

INTRODUCTION: WHY I CHOSE YOUTH MINISTRY

The essence of long-term youth ministry may have been best expressed by veteran youth worker Les Christie when he talked of being "buried with a Bible in one hand and a volleyball in the other."

There is something special about a job where you get paid to play. Where else could I influence young lives with the saving love of an awesome God, but also thoroughly trounce high school freshmen in one-on-one basketball?

And make no mistake about it, I pick my playmates carefully. There is no glory or pleasure in having some future Michael Jordan walk all over you. No sir. It's important for youth to have someone to look up to and model themselves after, so I make sure I'm abundantly better than the person I'm playing. (How could a kid look up to someone who was clutching his gut, gasping, "Wait a minute...time out...slow down"?)

Give me a double-left-footed, near-sighted klutz, and I'll teach him the meaning of important terms like determination, perseverance, and loser-buys-pizza.

Oh, I can hear the nay-sayers now: "What a terrible attitude! With the harsh realities of today's societal forces, the young person caught in the throes of adolescence absolutely requires adult leadership that offers a nurturing relationship to his or her extremely fragile self-image and self-esteem."

The only problem I have with statements like this is that they are usually made by somebody who wouldn't know a real-life, oh-shoot-I've-got-another-zit adolescent if one jumped off a skateboard and rammed an iPod down his or her throat.

The fact of the matter is that, because of "harsh realities" and "societal forces," the kids I'm working with better get toughened up. Nobody in the real world is going to kiss their boo-boos and say, "There, there, now...it will be all better."

So if it takes me whipping a few non-jocks at basketball to help them get a secure start into an uncertain future, who am I to deny them that privilege?

Of course, as I grow older, it's getting harder and harder to find students inept enough to make the cut. Maybe I should consider a ministry with preschoolers. ("Hey, Bobby! Wanna see me put this ball through that circle up there?")

A LESSON IN SPECIES IDENTIFICATION

There are certain islands on Planet Earth that are populated by unique members of the animal kingdom – citizens of creation that are not found anywhere else in the known universe. Australia, Tasmania, and the Galapagos Islands are the homes of animals and insects that have never seen the light of day on any mainland...apart from a zoo.

Which brings our attention to church secretaries.

The North American Church Secretary (NACS) is a blanket term that represents two distinct species: the Cherubic Miracle Worker and the Brimstone-Singed Squawker. While there are no consistent physical markings to help you distinguish between the two, there are a number of seemingly instinctual actions that will clue you into with which species of NACS you're dealing.

The Cherubic Miracle Worker is usually found sitting at her desk with a phone receiver propped in one ear, one hand taking notes, the other hand on the computer keyboard, while she collates a multi-page printing project with her feet. The CMW knows every church member's address, phone number, spiritual gifts, and soft drink preference. She's the person to call if you need to find out who's on what committee, how long they've served, or what they usually wear to meetings.

The Miracle Worker NACS not only has information, but she can use that information to produce meaningful reports – the shorter the advance notice, the quicker and more-accurate the resulting document.

It is no exaggeration to say that if this species of NACS suddenly got sick, got amnesia, or got hired away by some fancy computer software company that offers to pay her twelve times the salary the church gives her, the congregation she serves would come to a grinding, screeching, hair-on-the-back-of-the-neck-raising halt.

The Brimstone-Singed Squawker is also often seen with a phone to her ear, but the similarity to the Cherubic Miracle Worker ends there. Rather than answering questions or setting appointments, her phone conversations usually include personal information gleaned through the pastor's office door while he's having a counseling session with a distraught church member.

The BSS holds a power similar to the Cherubic Miracle Worker in that the volume of information within her control is massive. The difference is that the BSS holds that power in a death-grip; wields that power with frightening brutality. Do you need to make copies of an important hand-out for a Bible study? You better be on friendly terms with your Squawker secretary or you just might not be able to find a supply of paper. Do your evangelism plans call for a mailing to all the families on your mailing list? The speed at which it gets mailed will be in direct proportion to how long it's been since you've brought in a bag of bagels or brownies or one of those diamond-studded bracelets with a cachet of that generic designer-scent-rip-off cream stuff.

It is no exaggeration to say that the Brimstone-Singed Squawker has been partly responsible for the expansion of youth ministry. If it weren't for the BSS, North American Youth Ministers wouldn't have *near* the expertise in packing U-Hauls. Or half as much knowledge in geography. Or a third of their skills in learning new names and faces.

* * * * * * *

Don't misunderstand. A secretary won't usually spell the difference between your success and failure...but she will gladly tell you whether *you've* spelled it right.

PREACHERS

Preacher, pastor, reverend, evangelist, minister...whatever you call him, he is a different species than a youth minister. He may profess to be in the same boat, on the same battlefield, serving the same purpose as a youth minister, but there is a fundamental, seminal, even genetic difference between a youth minister and a preacher.

To be absolutely candid, preachers are missing a chromosome. From birth, they go through life lacking an element of human living that most of us take for granted: Preachers have no sense of humor.

I know, I know...some doofus is reading this and saying, "But *my* preacher has a sense of humor! He tells the best jokes." I encourage you, Mr./Mrs./Miss/Ms Doofus, to pay closer attention to those jokes. There aren't too many of them told outside the safe confines of a sermon illustration.

You see...preachers don't actually enjoy humor. They may use it to help break down communication barriers or to illustrate a point, but they don't enjoy humor for humor's sake. They just don't get it.

I take that back. They *do* get humor. They get it from a file folder or *Reader's Digest* or books like *Clean Jokes for Every Occasion, Vol. 4*. Very rarely will preachers see anything humorous arising out of real life experiences around them. "What could be funny about a Man Of God slaving for the Savior? This is serious business, and people won't take you seriously if you're perceived as a jester."

Which brings me to the point of this truth that is particularly relevant to you if you are a youth minister: Because of the preacher's total lack of a sense of humor, it will be physiologically impossible for him to understand or appreciate yours.

Don't take this fact lightly. It is something you'll have to live with your entire career. Every year, as you sit through an evaluation meeting, you'll hear variations on a theme: "I feel you need to work on being more sensitive about your humor." "One thing to have as a priority this year would be to watch out how you joke around." "I'm not sure everyone appreciates your humor." "I'm afraid we may be offending some people by the way we always crack jokes." (*"We?"* *"Always?"*)

Of course, the only logical way to deal with such myopic criticism is to look the critic in the face and nod while you go through next Sunday's lesson outline in your head. (You'll know when he's done. He'll stand up and offer to shake your hand.) The thought is not original with me, but it bears repeating: The key is sincerity. Once you learn how to fake that, everything else is a breeze.

* * * * * * *

This whole topic of how to handle preachers probably deserves its own chapter. Actually, it would take another book. Perhaps a series of books, like *Dummies for Dummies*. No, no, no . . . I've got it. A twelve volume, leather-bound *Encyclopedia of Interpersonal Relationships With*

People Who Think They Know Your Job Better Than You, But Really Have Never Been Within Spitting Distance Of A Clue.

When you get right down to it, it's pretty basic stuff. The most important thing to remember when dealing with preachers is to protect their self-image by letting them think they make a difference. As long as they believe they're being effective, they won't start suspiciously wondering why you have 112 kids involved in Bible study and he can only get 9 people to show up for Sunday night service.

ELDERS

Swimmers swim. Golfers golf. Party poopers – well, you get the idea. There is one life-impacting exception to the series, though. I hate to be the one to break the news to you, but I guess that's why they pay me the big bucks.

Okay. Here goes.

Elders do not eld.

Oh, it's not because they don't *want* to eld, or that they're *afraid* to eld. It's just that – well, since we're all friends here, I can be frank (Sometimes, I get a little tired of being Dewey, so it's refreshing to be Frank periodically.) – it's just that they don't know *how* to eld.

Now, as soon as I make a statement like that, some of you will think that I'm saying that all elders in local congregations are stupid. I am *not* saying that all elders in local congregations are stupid. I am saying that all elders in local congregations are ignorant.

Of course, you know that there's a difference between *stupid* and *ignorant*. The word *ignorant* comes to us from two Latin words: *igno*, which means to be oblivious to or unaware of something; and *rant*, which refers to the payment one makes to a landlord in exchange for the privilege of watching his real estate investment grow equity. Therefore, *ignorant* means to forget to make a payment toward your housing costs.

So...um...I guess what I'm saying is that elders are stupid.

But it's not their fault! It's not like there's a bunch of training out there. We can't send prospective elders to college to take *Elding 101*. I haven't seen any books on the shelves like *How To Eld On A Shoestring*, or *The 7 Habits Of Highly Effective Elders*. Sure, the Apostle Paul wrote some stuff about church leaders, but face it – he was pretty heavy on character traits and had precious little to say of a practical, dirt-under-the-fingernails nature.

So, we settle for people who own a business, or manage a business, or can spell "business" correctly 75% of the time. And that's where your problems as a youth minister will begin. That's the soil your problems will be planted in. That's the neglected sock drawer in which your problems will ferment.

Whatever you do, before you agree to become the youth minister at any church, check out what the elders do for a living. Avoid elderships led by men who own their own businesses. They will treat you like just another grunt employee. On the other hand, don't place yourself under an elder who is a grunt employee. He will take out his frustrations toward his boss on you. On the other hand, stay away from middle-management types. They'll whittle your grand plan for ministry into a list of visits made, lessons written, and wastebaskets emptied. On the other hand...you're way out of hands.

The real thing to do is to create enough paper so that the elders will be satisfied that you're doing something. If you keep them busy looking at retreat posters and pizza party receipts, they won't have time to meddle with your lesson content or Tetris score.

However, all bets are off when you find yourself in the worst of all possible youth ministry pickles: when a child of an elder is a member of the youth group. When this happens (which is not as often as you might think, since most elders' children are serving time in jail before they get their driver's licenses) you must treat the teen in question as you would a foreign agent.

I recommend bribes. A pre-paid calling card or permission to sneak some smokes onto the church bus will usually do the trick. Just take care of the needs of any elder's teen, and you'll have a long, bright future in youth ministry, my friend.

BUSSED OR BUST

It's a stereotypical scene. You've seen it in any number of movies or Saturday-morning cartoons. A group of people is hunched around a small-but-friendly fire. The sky is full of stars. The night is quiet except for the crackling of the flames and the voice of one person. That one person has the undivided attention of each soul around the campfire, not because that person is famous or physically attractive or handing out hundred-dollar bills, but because that lone voice is telling a...*Ghost Story*.

I've never been one to encourage interest in the occult or the psychic or the paralegal, but I have been known to stoop to the level of reciting "Give me back my golden arm" when the time was right.

When I started in Youth Ministry – back when hayrides were an exciting innovation that involved dodging piles of stegosaurus guano – I had to find my scary stories in old books and back copies of *People*. Now, of course, I've had enough life experiences of my own that I could write my own book full of Tales That Send Shivers Down Your Digestive Tract. [Note: I've got first dibs on this idea. You can't have it. You can't use it. You can't talk about it to your closest friend. In fact, now that you've found out about it, I'm afraid I'm going to have to kill you. How does a week from Tuesday work for you?]

If you stay in Youth Ministry long enough, you, too, will be able to relate stories of enough horror and suspense to keep children, teens, and adults checking under their cots and/or changing their shorts for months. You won't have to make up anything, and you won't have to talk about zombies, mummies, or IRS agents. All that will be necessary will be to tell about your experiences with your church bus.

Let the recounting of one of my experiences serve as an example:

We had spent an absolutely awesome week at a conference in central Indiana. The weather had been clear, the speakers understood English, and the food was non-toxic. [Note: That's about as much as you can hope for, you know?] On Saturday morning, we loaded up the bus and started the 600-mile trip back home.

Our first omen of things to come happened after our breakfast stop.

Everyone finished his or her Egg McMuffin and Coke and headed back out to the church bus. We counted heads to make sure we were all on board, turned the ignition, and spent the next hour-and-a-half trying to find the problem in our electrical system. It didn't help to try to jump-start the beast, so we eventually decided to push it up to speed and pop the clutch. [Note: This actually ended up being one of the most team-building experiences of the week. Especially when Josh Capucci tripped while he was pushing and got run over by the trailer we were hauling.]

We had gotten all of two miles down the road when someone said, "Where's Beth?" Well, Beth was back at McDonald's calling her dad (the senior pastor!) to find out the cell phone number of our bus driver so she could tell us to turn around. [Note: Always have someone with a cell phone with you on a trip in a church bus. It will come in handy to send for help and to keep updated on sport scores.]

On the road again, we traveled for several hours until the serpentine belt of the van that was following the bus snapped. [Note: We had the van following so it could go for help in case something went wrong with the bus. Who could have guessed that it would be the *bus* winding through a rural, Central Illinois town on a Saturday afternoon, looking for an auto parts store?]

Two hours later, we were finally cruising toward home.

Around midnight – seventeen hours into what was supposed to be a 15 hour trip – the bus' headlights went AWOL. [Note: I am *NOT* making this stuff up! This actually happened!] We pulled into a 24-hour truck stop/convenience store/disease emporium and began exorcising the electrical demons.

With 4-5 hours of driving still awaiting us, I started exploring our options for an overnight stay. There was a motel nearby, so I walked over to see how many rooms were available. The answer was easy to come up with, because the clerk only had to count to zero. [Note: This was quite fortunate, as that's probably about as high as the clerk could count, anyway.] There was a country music jamboree happening in Black Falls that weekend, and there were no rooms to be had anywhere within 37 miles of the place. However, after a couple phone calls to two different managers, we were offered the floor of the motel's conference room for *only* fifty dollars.

About that time, the motel's security guard said that we could probably stay at his church, which was only a couple miles down the road. [Note: In every good Ghost Story, there is at least one streak of light.]

Having determined that we were unable to fix the headlight problem, we followed the security guard to his church's building and camped out in their classrooms. After five hours of sleep and a breakfast of doughnuts and

Sunny Delight, we pushed the bus back to life and – once again – headed for home.

The morning's drive was going well. The sun was at our back, and a cooling sprinkle was keeping the summer heat at bay. It was God's way of letting us catch our breath before the final blow.

We were one mile away from the Minnesota border (and only 45 minutes from home) when the right rear tire of the bus bade a fond farewell to its tread. [Note: Have I mentioned that I am not making this up?] Now, one good thing about having trouble with a church bus is that it teaches you to prepare for trouble on the next trip. We had had a tire blow-out on a previous trip, so we were prepared with a spare this time around.

Just as we got the sleeping bags and suitcases out of the trailer (so we could get to the spare), the refreshing, light drizzle became a steady rain. One half-hour later, as we were putting the flat tire away, it really started to pour. When we finished putting the last suitcase back in the trailer, the thunder rolled. We were about to lay our hands on the bus and give it one more push-start when a bolt of lightning streaked from the sky and interfaced with our beloved mode of transportational frustration.

The engine of the bus roared into life. [Storytelling Note: At this point, insert a clip from *Frankenstein*..."It's alive! It's *alive!*"]

THE PHONE

For youth ministers with the mixed blessing of a secretary, there is one message from her that creates fear deep and dark: "I need to leave early/run to the office supply outlet/rebuild the engine in our sport utility vehicle, so could you catch the phone?"

Most people aren't aware of this, but there is a sensor-chip within all modern business phones that creates an electrical impulse vacuum whenever a secretary leaves her desk for more than 5.7 minutes. What this does is actually *attract* telephone calls when the secretary "steps out for a few minutes."

So...no matter how quiet things have been all day, about six minutes after the secretary leaves early/runs to the office supply outlet/starts to rebuild the engine in her sport utility vehicle, the phone begins to ring with a regularity and rapidity that rivals quartz crystals.

A lot of the calls are easy to handle. Well, some of the calls are easy to handle. Actually, just a few of the calls. Okay, okay...the point-oh-seven percent of the calls that are wrong numbers are easy to handle.

Most of the time.

Once, a woman almost had me convinced that I was her nephew, Lamont. It was a good thing she finally realized she'd dialed wrong. I had started planning what to buy her for Christmas.

Other semi-easy calls are the ones where people are asking for information about the church: "What time are your services?" "Do you have a nursery?" "Does your preacher wear a Rolex?"

I must admit, though, that even these info-seeking calls can be tricky. How do you briefly answer questions like, "What does your church believe?" (The Bible.); "Are your people friendly?" (It depends on whether it's Mother's Day or the middle of a four-part series on stewardship.); or, "Can God make a rock so big that ---" (Never mind.)

But requests for information are nothing compared to the timid-voiced caller who says, "I need to talk to a minister." Hoo-boy, now *there's* a call you should avoid at all costs.

I know what you're thinking: "Wait a minute, Mr. Servant-Of-All-In-The-Name-Of-Christ. Didn't you enter The Ministry to comfort the afflicted and support the down-trodden? Aren't you supposed to deny yourself, take up your cross, and all that jazz? Where's your compassion, man!?"

I'm not sure, but I think I lost it the first time an anonymous caller asked me to pray for her step-daughter's former husband's nephew's cat, which had been possessed by the spirit of the anti-Christ and was sending subliminal messages to her through her microwave.

* * * * * * *

The final two categories of callers are not so much difficulties as they are time-wasting annoyances: salespeople and chatty church members.

In actuality, salespeople from the different religious publishing houses can be about the easiest callers to handle. There is a very simple technique to use that has proven very effective for scores of highly successful youth ministry professionals: say yes to every question they ask.

No, really…I mean it. It works!

A sample dialogue:

"Good morning! My name is Jason, and I'm with Especially Youth Group Publishing. Are you Pastor Ross?" *Yes.* [The degree of truth in your responses is not the issue here. What matters is applying the "yes technique" consistently, and thereby reducing confusion and shortening your time wasted on actually conversing with a salesperson.]

"Well, Pastor Ross, I hope you're having a great day in the Lord. Is the weather treating you right up there?" *Yes.* [The degree of truth in your responses is not the issue here.]

"Well good. Do you have three minutes you could give me?" *Yes.* [The degree of truth in your responses....]

"Pastor Ross, would you agree with me that one of the hardest challenges young people face today is knowing what's right and what's wrong in relation to drugs and alcohol?" *Yes.* [The degree of truth....]

"And I'm sure that you are always looking for teaching materials that will tell teenagers what to think. Am I right?" *Yes.* [The degree....]

"Pastor Ross, Especially Youth Group Publishing has come up with just the thing you've been looking for. Would you be interested in taking a 30-day-same-as-cash look at it?" *Yes.* [The....]

Do you see how it works? Instead of trying to correct any of the erroneous statements Jason made, and forcing him to go to Plan B of his scripts, I have taken him with great haste to the point in his call where he can verify my address, hang up, and leave me alone. (Which was my greatest desire all along.)

If you've been paying attention, you realize that I now have to deal with the fact that Jason actually believes I'm interested in his stuff and is sending me a sample of everything in the warehouse. Not to worry. When the secretary returns from leaving early/running to the office supply outlet/rebuilding the engine in her sport utility vehicle, she can send it all back with a note explaining that the material doesn't meet our present needs but that we'll keep Jason's phone number on file. [The degree of truth....]

* * * * * * *

Perhaps the hardest call of all to deal with is the one that comes from a church member who really called to tell the secretary something, but decides to ask how things are with you anyway. I don't know if it's a warped sense of manners that doesn't allow the person to pass a chance to have a polite conversation, or whether the caller has no life and craves human contact, even over the phone. What I *do* know is that these chewers-of-the-fat are the biggest drain of time and the hardest to get rid of.

It's not that I don't know *how* to get rid of them. There's any number of ways to bring the call to a halt. It's just that I don't know how to get rid of them and keep my job.

For instance, an effective technique would be to start saying, "What? Hello? Are you still there?" while the caller is yammering away about the weather or road conditions or the consistency of the communion bread. For a salesperson or an information-seeker, this would allow you to hang up and get on with answering the other calls coming in. But the talkative church member won't let it go at that. He/She will call back to see if the phones are really out of order. This makes the situation even drearier, because now the caller actually has something to talk about.

Or worse yet, the caller will contact a church trustee to tell him about "the problem with the church phone," and you'll end up having to explain about the whole deceitful mess and word will get back to the caller and he/she will be hopelessly offended and start rallying for a confidence vote on your continued employment at the church...at which point you might as well start gassing up the U-Haul.

So, what's to be done?

When the secretary has to leave early/run to the office supply outlet/rebuild the engine in her sport utility vehicle, insist that you go along/push the shopping cart/carry her wrenches.

An ounce of prevention is worth a pound of cure.

STANDING OUT IN THE CROWD

If you want to see the latest clothing styles that are being embraced by America's teenagers; if you want to experience today's hottest music; if you want to know exactly how to trim your facial hair so as to blend in with the funkiest of the funky...the place to be is a National Youth Workers Convention.

Convention is not really an accurate word for a gathering of professional and volunteer youth-worker-type-people. Since the inception of youth ministry (back when Elisha called a pair of bears out of the woods to practice Tough Love on some snotty-nosed street punks who had called him "Baldy"), the adults involved in leading young people to a relationship with God have taken an almost Shiite-level of pride in being *un*conventional. They *desire* to be different.

You can tell youth workers really, really want to be different by the fact that they all look alike.

Now of course, in different decades there are different looks, but at any given moment there is a fairly uniform code of appearance that sets youth workers apart from the tradition-bound, don't ever-stand-out, gee-I-hope-I-blend-in-and-nobody-notices-me pew-sitters.

When I began in youth work, the rage was v-neck camel hair tunics, with bones braided in our hair. Later on, the pseudo-hippie style of well-worn jeans, sandals, and a guitar was *de rigueur*. At the time of this writing, 93.7% of all youth workers have a mustache and goatee.

This most recent bit of peer group identification is especially controversial with the 23% of youth workers who are female.

Having such a homogenous appearance is very helpful. When a church does the old fire-this-guy-and-hire-another-one routine every two to three years, the teens don't really have to deal with much of a change. That helps them feel secure. It also helps to keep the congregation's pictorial directory from becoming outdated.

I'm not sure *how* the "uniform of the day" is decided upon. I suspect there are meetings in Nashville involving all the folks who are scheduled to do styling and make-up for the next *Mercy Me* project:

"Oh, Tiffany, bring over that hair dye catalog!"

"What do you think? Can we get any more mileage out of body piercing?"

"What about that balding guy in Minnesota? What could we do to make him seem more out-of-it?"

"Impossible task, Anton."

MY SPACE

A man's home may be his castle. In fact, it's very likely, modern plumbing and insulation not withstanding, that a man's home *can* rightly be considered his castle; his refuge; his tax-deductible-interest generator of to-do lists.

Not so with a youth minister's office.

A youth minister's office doesn't protect him from anything. The door is never locked, the phone is never off the hook, and often the window looks out onto a parking lot.

All things considered, a youth minister's office is very little like a castle and very much like an unclaimed-freight distribution center.

Take my own office.

Please.

It started off being neat and organized, yes indeed. I moved in with my books, my knickknacks, and a filing-cabinet-full of college class notes and magazine articles that haven't been exposed to fresh air since they were encased in manila card stock...about the same time Ben Franklin was inventing the electronic hair-perm. There was a place for everything, and everything in its place.

And then it began. Slowly. With the outer appearance of innocence, it began. My office was incrementally transformed from a place of order and control to a place of chaos and unbridled matter multiplication.

First it was a letter that I needed to respond to, so I couldn't file it. It was laid – lain? – *placed* on a corner of my desk. Then there was the packet of curriculum materials that I needed to pretend to review before sending it back. I put it on the empty bookshelf to the right of my desk.

So far, so good, but then the youth group went on a retreat and I'm now holding two sleeping bags for their forgetful owners. An ex-leader of a Campus Life club was cleaning out his closet and thought I might want some of his books from the Fifties on how to organize wiener roasts. The church was given five boxes of 3-ring binders that the youth could *surely* use. The T-shirts for Vacation Bible School have arrived, and I've just been told that the crew working on expanding our parking lot needs a place to store their grater.

Somewhere in here are my notes for tonight's lesson.

THE R. T. O. T. M.

Time is such a novel concept. We can't see it, so it's hard to define. We can't control it, so we at least try to measure it. But then, how do you measure something when you don't even know what it is? It's the stuff our lives use as currency, but nobody owns any.

And who needs Einstein's Theory of Relativity to know that time is not constant? Any youth minister worth his or her T-shirt collection could tell you *that*! In fact, being, myself, worth a T-shirt or two, I've formalized an important tool in understanding Time that I humbly call the "Roth Theory Of Time Multiplicity."

The RTOTM states, "For any given event, there are at least three distinct, separate, and mutually exclusive moments in time."

For instance:

1) the registration deadline you set

2) the date you actually need the registrations

3) the date the teens turn in the registrations

If you noticed a progression in that list, you are to be applauded for your wisdom and insight. But don't get a big head about it. You still have to figure out how to align the planets so that No. 3 comes somewhere in the same month as No. 2.

It's not that teens *can't* comply with deadlines, it's just that the minister before you trained them to *ignore* deadlines. He or she would set some ridiculously early registration deadline (like, say, two hours before an event) and then, when the church bus got flagged down twenty minutes after it left by a frantic parent with a pleading teen, instead of taking the proper course of action and throwing the whining, little pansy out on his/her ear (along with his/her teen), the rube actually let the late-comer join the trip.

[PLEASE NOTE: If you are the first youth minister at your location, you can conveniently blame the parents instead of "the former minister."]

And it's not just registration deadlines. The Roth Theory Of Time Multiplicity applies to departure times:

1) the time-to-leave you set

2) the time you actually need to leave

3) the time the church bus gets started

4) the time you actually leave

5) the time the teens show up

[Of course, in this progression, sometimes No.'s 4 and 5 are reversed. If you don't want to drive an empty bus, you will probably *always* reverse No.'s 4 and 5.]

But all right, already. Enough complaining. My general policy is that the only people who have a right to bellyache about something are those who know a better way or those who have had lunch at Papa Pedro's Taco Town. In this particular case, I happen to be one of the former.

So what's to be done? How does the modern youth minister break the stranglehold apparent in the RTOTM?

Plan your work, and work your plan.

"Huh?"

Stop letting the irresponsible and untimely decisions and actions of teens (and their parents) control your ministry. Set your deadlines and don't accept any registrations after they pass. Announce your departure time and leave when you say you will.

Will this change things? Will this counteract the RTOTM?

Well . . . no.

But you'll wind up going to some swell concerts and conferences without having to worry about transporting a bunch of teenagers.

FEEDING THE FLOCK

Because one of Jesus' areas of growth involved his physicality, ("Jesus grew in wisdom and *stature,* and in favor with God and men." *Luke 2:52*) it is perfectly acceptable to include physical health and growth as part of your ministry with youth. In fact, you will be *expected* to provide for their physical well-being – specifically, their dietary needs – anytime you have a group of teens in captivity for more than forty-five minutes. Because of this, it behooves every youth minister to educate him/herself in the fundamentals of food.

As any true connoisseur of gastronomy knows, there are four basic food groups: sugar, caffeine, grease, and salt. These four substances, when ingested in the proper balance with each other, are sufficient to provide all the necessary energy, skin oil, and intestinal disruption to fully function in adolescent society. Without a minimal level of the Basic Four, a teenager would not be able to produce the vital levels of fidgeting, acne, and flatulence it takes to be recognized as one-of-the-gang.

Your job, as a minister of the gospel of Christ to the future movers and shakers of Planet Earth, is to provide the delicate balance of the Basic Four in forms that are both appetizing and numerous.

Now, don't get overly distraught at the immensity of your task. It is really a simple thing, and there is practically an infinity of ready-made products that will, as they say, fill the bill. (They will also fill stomachs and drain your budget.)

Sugar and Caffeine

The first two of the Basic Four are generally found together in an array of foods (as are the last two), so we can easily deal with them at the same time. The beauty of these two is that, not only are they available in the finger foods (candy, cookies, pudding) so popular with those of us who are too lazy – ahem-excuse me – busy to wash utensils, but also in beverages that come in easy-to-leave-behind cans.

An especially recommended S&C chewable is a fudge brownie. These little wonders pack the double-whammy of sugar AND caffeine in a nice, easy-to-inhale size. It's best to get them while they're still warm so they can be properly wadded up for the most efficient swallowing. An unrelated side benefit is that the leftover brownies can be used as substitute hockey pucks and/or driveway gravel.

The potent potables are obvious: Coke, Pepsi, Dr. Pepper and all their flavored and generic cousins. (You will notice that diet drinks are not mentioned. Only geeks and super-models drink diet soda.) Worthy of separate mention is the King of all teen-oriented liquids, Mountain Dew. What the discovery of PMS was for chronically cranky females, the invention of Mountain Dew was for hyperactive teenagers: it gave them an excuse for being the way they are. (Don't burst the teens' bubbles by telling them that the Dew still has less caffeine than coffee.)

Salt and Grease

While many foods contain salt, grease, and salt & grease, for the youth minister's purpose there are really only two: chips and pizza. Both rank extremely high in convenience and teen acceptance.

Outside of letting them get wet, it's pretty hard to go wrong with chips. Whether it's potato, corn, or tortilla, just open a bag and stand out of the way. And I do mean stand out of the way. During my first year of youth ministry I made the mistake of opening a bag of Doritos and bending down to pick one up off the floor. I spent the remainder of that party in a permanent toe-touch, and the rest of that year in traction.

And then there's pizza: the perfect food. It's been said that pizza is like sex: even when it's not great, it's not bad.

There is an art to ordering pizza for a whole group of kids, though. If you don't do it right, you could very quickly be in some of the deepest doo-doo you've ever feared. The first step is to do it yourself. Don't ask for anybody's opinion, suggestion, or help. (All you need from anybody else is cold, hard cash.) The minute you let somebody in on the process they'll think they're going to get the kind of pizza they want, and that almost never happens. Besides, if there are twelve people in the group, there will be at least eight different kinds of pizza requested. Trust me, OYOP! (Order Your Own Pizza)

Step two in group pizza procurement is ordering the right amount. One large pizza for every four teens works well, except if you have Junior High boys, in which case double the number . . . and make them thick crust.

Deciding what toppings to put on the pizzas is step three. I always keep it very simple. This keeps the cost down, plus, those are the kinds of pizzas I like the best. (Who's making the decisions around here, anyway?)

As when serving chips, try not to let your hand stray too near the pizza when it first arrives. If you don't believe me, ask my youth minister friend, Lefty.

* * * * * * *

And there you have it, the secret to your success. You can prepare so-so sermons and people will politely tell you it was a fine job. You can present lackluster lessons and the kids will still come so they can sleep on their friend's shoulder. You can facilitate dreary discussions and folks will be understanding and forgiving. But if you try serving radishes and fruit trays at a Senior High social, you better have your resume up-to-date.

LOCK-INS

I hate lock-ins. You know, of course, what I mean by *lock-in*: spending an entire night – all the way until morning – in the church building with the youth group kids plus the fringe friends who would usually never show up in a church building except on a court-induced, juvenile detention work-release program.

Of course, on the surface, it seems like a great idea. How else will you ever get some meaningful contact with those fringe kids? What better way to get some "relationship building" and "quality time" accomplished? After all, just considering time-with-the-teens, one lock-in equals 10-12 Sunday Schools!

WARNING! This line of reasoning will lead you down a steep and slippery path toward an early demise ... or worse.

* * * * * * *

A person could list practically any number of reasons to hate lock-ins. It would be enough to point out that God did not intend for humans to deprive themselves of sleep. Of course, the solution to that is to put sleep time in the lock-in's schedule. Of course, that doesn't work. If you schedule time for people to sleep, you will spend that entire time, of course, telling kids to be quiet and looking for the few who have sneaked out to the church bus to see just how many windows they can fog up at once. Of course, the solution to that is to just plan to stay up all night. Of course, that doesn't work. If you plan for everyone to stay up all night, there will be a full 27.8% of the participants who HAVE to sleep because they've got a big game the next day or their family is going to have a special memorial service for their ex-neighbor's in-law's former paper boy's dead preying mantis. Of course.

* * * * * * *

That's one of the things I hate about lock-ins. No matter what you do, it's not the right thing.

If you give the kids plenty of free time so they can talk with their friends and play board games, you will face two situations. One: Every 3.7 minutes, a Nintendo-deprived adolescent will engage his or her well-practiced whine and intone, "This is bo-ring!" Two: The windows of the church bus will get fogged up.

Of course, if you schedule activities to solidly fill each available minute, you will face the same two situations.

If you furnish the sugar, caffeine, grease, and salt (disguised as snack food, of course) that it would take to keep a Roman legion on the march, there won't be anything that anybody likes.

Of course, if you tell the teens to bring their own snacks to share, you'll end up getting a bag of Doritos, half-dozen brownies, and three cans of Mountain Dew.

If you plan a Bible study, the kids will want to just play.

Of course, if you plan to just play, the kids will complain that it was a waste of time because there was no Bible study.

Of course.

* * * * * * *

What it comes down to is a twelve-hour-long battle of wills:

- Will I make it through the night without collapsing?

- Will the snacks hold out?

- Will enough kids actually play the group games to make the name "group game" appropriate?

- Will we stop the couples fogging up the church bus windows before it's too late?

- Will anyone squeal on me if I duct-tape that kid to a chair and throw him into a closet until morning?

Of course, none of these things represent my real reason for hating lock-ins. Actually, I hate lock-ins because they turn me into a liar.

Of course, you're wondering how lock-ins turn me into a liar.

At the end of every lock-in I've ever been involved with, I have, without exception, made an official self-proclamation: "I am never going to do another lock-in."

Of course, about nine months later some eighth-grader says, "When are we going to have another lock-in? The last one we had was so FUN!"

And so, my resolve crumbles and I do whatever it takes to get kids to associate "church" with "excitement."

Of course.

YOU MAY BE SEATED

L ean to the left! Lean to the right! Stand up, sit down, fight, fight, fight! Not that I'm condoning violence, by any means. I'm just warning you that it could happen. And when it does, it could very well be centered on the "sit down" portion of the preceding cheer.

There's a whole cultural psychology about where a teenager sits in relation to others in his/her peer group that merits intensive study. In fact, our crack team of researchers and investigators are, at this very moment, thoroughly examining the topic over lunch at Bandito's Restaurante Del Mexicano and have documented some significant findings pertinent to different aspects of parking one's posterior.

In Youth Group Meetings

Posture. Using the term "posture" loosely, you will notice a uniform posture with your teens. Male or female, middle schooler or graduating senior...there is no difference. 85% of your youth group will sit in a curved-back, hunched-over pantomime of someone trying to get over a bad case of constipation.

For females, this "stance" comes from leaning toward each other and talking...which, of course, is their prime motivation for attending any function. If they can't talk to one another, or if they anticipate that there will be no one present they want to talk to, color them gone.

For the males in the group, this body configuration is necessary for the successful execution of the required balance-on-the-back-two-legs-of-the-chair maneuver. This particular exercise is *so* pervasive, in fact, that if you see one of your male teens *not* sitting like this, you can be sure that you're dealing with one of two things: 1) a Grade A, Government-Certified Doink; or 2) someone who needs to carefully concentrate because he has a bad case of the opposite-of-constipation.

Placement of Chairs. Back when the Earth's crust was still cooling and I first got into youth ministry, teens were expected to sit in chairs that were placed in neat, straight rows; facing the front of the room and eagerly awaiting wisdom to be imparted from the teacher.

Somewhere about the time Dr. McCoy first proclaimed that he was a doctor and not a stone mason, someone decided that group discussion was more important than wisdom impartation. With that change in focus came a change in seating arrangement. Placing all the chairs in one big circle became all the rage. It also spurred many a youth minister into a rage. In this new arrangement, the class clown could now not only distract the people sitting around him, but with very little effort could disrupt the whole group.

Next came the drive toward smaller discussion and task groups, resulting in a room full of 4-and-5-chair circles. This also resulted in at least half the people in the room with their backs toward the leader at all times.

What's the solution? Here's a hint: you wouldn't have to worry about how to arrange the chairs if you didn't *have* any chairs. [*Pass the tortilla chips, please.*]

Gender Interaction. By the looks of most youth groups, you'd think we were all Quakers...men on one side, women on the other. The only difference is the presence in the center of the room of the Couple-of-the-Month. (A rotating arrangement of who's dating whom in the youth group.)

What with the legendary hormone levels wafting around in the average youth group, the whole gender segregation thing is pretty surprising. You would think that you would have to police them and the location of their hands at all times. While this is true in less-formal situations like lock-ins, hayrides, and funeral visitations, something about a class or worship time changes all the rules of teendom. Rumor has it that it has something to do with the guys playing basketball before they come in to the youth group, but our researchers haven't been able to get close enough to confirm that as of this writing.

When Traveling

Whether traveling by bus, van, car pool or Disney's monorail, there is an extreme importance placed upon who-gets-to-sit-where. From the first cry of "Shotgun!" to the last slamming of the vehicle door, it's a contest worthy of Eric Liddell. Our team of investigators will be looking into this phenomenon as soon as they file their report on the pecking order of chickens. [*Where's the salsa?*]

Howdy Doody and Buffalo Bob had their Peanut Gallery, and all churches have their Teen Sections. Oh, they aren't specifically labeled as such or cordoned off for that purpose, but they are functionally unavailable for occupation by anyone over the age of twenty.

There are two schools of thought regarding this phenomenon. One says that it's wonderful to even have the precious children inside the walls of the church building and that we should be grateful that the Dear Ones like being together to worship Our-Lord-and-Savior-Jesus-Christ. The other goes something like, "All those ruffians are doing is talking and distracting one another and everyone around them. Why don't they sit with their parents or go outside?"

As with most two-sided opinions, there is a middle ground that is better by far. There needs to be a way to celebrate the presence of teens in our worship services and yet expect, encourage, and even assure decent and respectful behavior.

And as with most needs in our lives, someone has devised a way to make money from it.

For a fee considerably smaller than the national debt, Floyd Wescott, of Wabash, Indiana (the nation's first electrically-lit town!) will equip the seats/pews in your church's Peanut Gallery with the Behavior Response Alert Pew Program (BRAPP!) Each seat in your Teen Turf will be wired so as to administer a small-but-effective electric shock at the touch of a button. Is Tiffany talking to Amanda about her date? ZAP! Is Brad falling asleep? ZING! Are Josh and Joel running a lottery based on how many times the preacher uses the word "finally"? ZORCH!

Well...the double-bean burritos are here. I mean, um, our investigative team has exhausted not only the mild salsa, but also the research budget. [*I knew I should have just ordered water.*]

THE BIG L

In a world full of variation, diversity, and pizza joints, there is one aspect of being a youth minister that is common to all who wear the name. No matter how else they may differ from each other, there is a common issue to all. They can be male or female; young or old. Their skin can be white, brown, black, yellow, or fuchsia. They can be born in the U.S.A. or in Cucamonga. They can like Coke or Pepsi, pepperoni or plain cheese, Laurel or Hardy...It just doesn't matter!

All youth ministers have to deal with lust.

It is such a universal truth that one speaker (in the days when being a Youth Minister meant being a male) commented, "You can tell you've been in the ministry for a long time when you stop being attracted to the girls in your youth group and start thinking their moms look pretty good."

[At this point, I should apologize for writing about lust from a male perspective, but they say you should write about what you know, you know? Go with your strengths, I always say.]

The problem with this issue – besides it being, like, you know, a *sin* and all – is that youth ministry creates so *many* situations where the big L can rear – er, I mean raise – um, that is, *lift* its ugly head. [...and stare you down, roaring and baring – er, I mean exposing – um, that is, *showing off* its razor-sharp fangs.]   What with swimming parties, late-night road trips, and breathing, the decks are really stacked against you – er, I mean danger is built into – um, that is, it's an uphill struggle to keep your mind pure.

While the majority of the blame for all this must most assuredly rest on the smooth, white shoulders of each individual youth minister, there are two types of girls that present a particular problem to the YM who struggles with lust, *i.e.*, all of us:

1)   girls that have no idea they're tempting us;

2)   girls that have *every* idea about tempting us.

There is a type of female that is so absolutely unaware of herself that she could never conceive – er, I mean fantasize – um, that is, even *imagine* that her youth minister would in any way find her attractive. This is the gal who comes out of the shower asking if you've seen her towel. This is the young woman who slurps on a Popsicle® as it slowly drips down her chin. This is the female that I had better stop thinking about this very instant.

There is another category of girl that is *very* aware of her body and uses it to her advantage. This is the one who purposely brushes against you on her way to get dessert at camp. This is the temptress who wears low-cut tops and bends over a lot. Okay, I admit it, this is the girl who doesn't *really* exist, but guys like to think she does.

Most people think you need to keep any struggle like this a secret -- don't let anyone know you think about sex with anything other than disdain. I have found, however, that admitting to the big L has done wonders for my standing with my discipleship group of 8th- and 9th-grade boys. ("You mean you're *not* dead from the neck down?") Being considered an actual member of the human race does wonders for discussions.

However, caution must be used when broaching the subject of lust. While it's usually a good idea to call things by their proper names, guys have a tendency to lose track of what you're saying once you use the word "breast." I made the mistake of using that word once while sharing a prayer request about my wife's fight against that particular type of cancer. Bless their hearts, the guys *wanted* to be serious and concerned...but it was a week-and-a-half before I could get anything out of them other than glassy-eyed stares and a bit of drool at the corners of their mouths. Besides, you don't need to get graphic in your descriptions of what a person lusts about...the teens understand what you mean – all too well. Just mention the girl looking for her towel and you'll have discussion material to last a lifetime.

CONCERTS

From time to time, you will become enamored with the deep, thoughtful lyrics of some Contemporary Christian artist and desire above all else to expose the students to them with the impact of a live performance. You will go temporarily insane and believe in your heart of hearts – contrary to all logical lines of reasoning and flying in the face of all reasonable lines of logic – that it would benefit the teens in your care to attend a concert together.

You will be gravely mistaken.

The first mistake will be your thought that "the youth group" will be attending the concert together. You will *plan* for a large portion of the group to go. You will *expect* a large portion of the group to go. You will not *experience* a large portion of the group going.

You may understandably ask, "Why is this so?"

The answer is two-fold:

1) For them to go to the concert, they would have to make plans prior to five minutes before departure time. This is asking WAY too much of them and placing undue stress into their fragile lives.

2) None of their friends will be going, because there aren't any Christian musicians that wear their underwear on the outside of their clothing and/or spit fake blood. And of course, if the friends ain't goin', ain't NObody goin'.

* * * * * *

Because of your false expectation of participation, and because you want to save a few bucks for everybody, you will take advantage of the concert promoter's offer of a group discount. That means two things:

1) You will have to purchase a minimum of about 47 tickets to qualify as a "group."

2) You will have to purchase the tickets long before you get any kind of commitment from the kids.

If you've been following closely, you are realizing right about now that your course of action has caused you to become encased in a preserved cucumber. In other words, you're in a pickle. You've got 47 tickets to a concert that 3 students have decided to think about attending.

So, what do you do? You've got to get rid of these tickets SOMEhow!

1) You try to encourage your teens to invite their friends. You offer half-price or even free tickets if they're for unchurched students. This results in additional sales of zero. The reason for this is simple, as explained by Stu "Jiggy" Pullman (an elder's kid): "I'm so sure I'm gonna ask a friend of mine to sit through some lame concert by a band neither one of us have ever heard of!"

2) You call up the other Youth Ministers in your area and offer them the extra tickets at the Reduced Group Rate. This results in additional sales of zero, too, because all the other Youth Ministers in the area have done the same thing you did and were just about to call YOU with a ticket offer.

3) You give the tickets to students as door prizes at youth group meetings leading up to the concert date. This moves tickets out the door, but it doesn't increase attendance at the concert, because when the tickets move out the door they promptly find their way to the sidewalk or parking lot or glove compartment of a parent's car – mixed in with the extra napkins from Wendy's and an 8-track of Marty Robbins' greatest hits.

* * * * * * *

Eventually, the day of the concert comes. You load up all the kids into your Geo Metro (with room left over), and head out to the concert venue. Depending on the popularity of the artist in question, this could be either another, larger church in the area, a stadium from which the hockey crowd has just cleared, or the garage of the Senior Pastor's pool boy.

You find a place to park, sign over your firstborn male child to the parking attendant, and walk the 47 blocks back to the concert location.

Now, if you're lucky, you've chosen to go to a concert that has reserved seating. This saves you the embarrassment of having the teens you've brought with you go running off the second you get inside – to get "good seats" – and you not seeing them again until you post their bail at the county lock-up. With reserved seating, you can go directly to your seats and become intimately familiar with the pole you're sitting behind.

The concert itself is a novel experience. Which is to say, you might as well take along a novel to read, because you won't be able to glean any meaningful content from the music or the between-song chatter. The music, with those lyrics that drew you to the idea of bringing your students to the concert in the first place, is loud and energetic and unintelligible. This doesn't bother the assembled crowd, though, because they are all busy talking and going back and forth to the concession stands and the rest rooms.

What the artist says in-between songs doesn't matter either. With any word coming out of his/her mouth, the crowd will yell and scream its approval:

1) "Are you ready to have a good time?" Yeah! Woo-hoo!

2) "Jesus is so cool!" Yeah! Woo-hoo!

3) "Cough-Gasp-Hack!" Yeah! Woo-hoo!

This fact, if you are at all sensitive, will royally hack you off. Here's this – this – this *musician* getting instantaneous positive feedback for every stray comment coming out of his/her mouth, and you can't get anybody to listen to a message that you spend 2 months preparing.

The good news in all of this – the thing saving you from a life of bitterness – Is the fact that you won't actually be inside listening to the concert. Noooo…. You'll be out on the sidewalk, getting to know other youth ministers from the area while you all try to sell off your leftover tickets.

PERSONAL VISITS WITH TEENS

It is impossible to effectively minister to youth from behind a desk. (Unless, of course, your desk is small enough that you can sit behind it but still reach a kid to box his ears a good one.) From time to time, you simply must have some personal contact with the teens in your charge...go figure.

This personal contact can come in many forms: a shared moment in the church hallway, letters of encouragement, or driving really slowly past their houses late at night while you stare in their windows. Sooner or later, though, you will need to spend some one-on-one time with the students by scheduling personal visits.

When I was starting out in youth ministry, this was easily accomplished by just dropping by a kid's place and asking to see him/her: "Oh sure, he's out back mending the pterodactyl net. Let me call him for you. Zantar! Oongalluh!"

Nowadays, it can be a little more complicated. You usually have to call several days in advance to get on the waiting list for the student's appointment secretary, who will call you back in 48 to 96 hours with a short list of available time slots. These time slots will be 15 to 20 minutes long, nestled away between soccer practices, speech competitions, and unicycle lessons.

Once you've traversed the scheduling obstacle course and secured a time slot in the teen's life, you'll need a plan. You can't just walk in and say, "How's it going?" Remember that you have to compete with all the other *important* things on the student's plate, so don't come across as some lame combination of Mister Rogers and cottage cheese.

An opening salvo of compliments and encouragement will help weaken the enemy's – er – the student's defenses: "Hey, Derek, you're looking good! Nice SUV in the driveway. You ever let your folks drive it? Hey, by the way, excellent job getting by security at the last lock-in, man! You could hold seminars!"

Just in case this doesn't open a line of conversation/bragging by the student in question, you need to have a selection of ice-breaker questions in your head; ready to use to get a conversation going or to keep one from sinking towards death. Here's a short list of field-tested questions that are guaranteed to open a door into any teen's heart:

1) What do you think about the way things are going at church?

2) How often do you pray?

3) Do you know that God loves you and has a wonderful plan for your life?

4) If you were to die today, what would you say to God if He asked you, "Why should I let you into My heaven?"

5) Can you loan me fifty bucks?

If this fails to fill up the twenty-minute audience you've been granted, you can always challenge the student to some sort of competition. Video games are the best bet. They won't involve any actual sweat on your part, plus, you will be thoroughly trounced…giving the teen in question an adrenaline rush that will be associated with your visit and lead to a favorable response when the elders ask him/her how he/she feels about you/your ministry.

That *is*, after all, the real goal of personal visits: keeping the elders off your back. That student doesn't need you to visit. Students have plenty of friends to hang out with. What do they need some fossil coming around for? No, no, no…the reason you must go to all this time, trouble, and embarrassment is to make a favorable impression upon those who decide whether you stay or go away. If you log in a truckload of such visits every month, the elders will be so impressed with your self-sacrifice (since they can't *imagine* spending time talking to a teen without waggling a finger at them) that they will renew your contract on the spot.

Being able to put off that call to U-Haul for another year is always a good thing.

NO ~~MAN'S~~ ELDER'S LAND

L et us turn our attention to that area of youth ministry responsibility that strikes fear into the hearts of all the blue-haired ladies within a two-mile radius of your church building: The Youth Room.

Often referred to as "In There," (as in, "No way. I'm not going *in there* without back-up.") there are a number of reasons why the older adults in your church fear that room or hallway or closet-sized stall designated for use by the teens in your charge:

1) One could conceivably encounter an actual teenager within the youth room.

2) Unpleasant memories of one's own high school years are too much to face.

3) It's hard to tell what kind of active cultures are at work in that stuff under the couch.

* * * * * * *

A few years ago, one of the definitely-over-65 crowd was on his way to the utility closet to find some duct tape to repair the handle of his 4-legged cane and he accidentally entered The Youth Room. There was instant silence as every adolescent in the place turned and stared at the strange sight of a barely-mobile man trying to back away quietly, but all the while slipping in the puddle he had left on the floor when the shock of his mistake emptied his bladder: he looked like a long-retired Michael Jackson impersonator doing an extremely slow moonwalk.

The proof of my success at having turned those teens into actual disciples was the fact that none of them burst into laughter until after the gentleman had gotten down the hallway and around the corner.

The Furniture

The interiors of youth rooms are just as varied as the living rooms of the members of the congregation you serve. To be more precise, your youth room will look a lot like what your congregants' living rooms looked like five years ago. To be totally exact, the furniture in your youth room will consist of the cast-offs and garage sale rejects from everyone in your church who has remodeled their homes.

The youth room at a church I used to serve was the repository for two couches, a love seat, a La-Z-Boy, three coffee tables, and a video arcade model of Pac-Man. Now, before you start drooling in envy, let me explain that the couches were also home to a well-established colony of fleas, the love seat had several stains of questionable origin, the La-Z-Boy was permanently reclined, the three coffee tables only had a total of eight legs, and the arcade game console was missing its joystick. On top of all that, the room itself was only ten by twelve feet, so there was a total of 7 square inches of floor space left without something on it.

Come to think of it, though, it was probably a good thing that the floor was hidden by all the furniture. That way, no one could see the hodge-podge collection of carpet samples that Deacon Foster had donated when his carpet store went out of business. (If those samples represented the best of his stock, there was no mystery as to why the store went belly-up.)

The Sound System

In order to introduce your charges to the plethora of Christian music artists available for their ignoring, your youth room needs to be equipped with an adequate sound system. Said sound system should somewhat simulate symphonic harmonics, plus the pure, painful power of rock arena decibels. If your woofers and tweeters don't woof and tweet with significant Richter scale registration, you might as well be playing *Lawrence Welk in a Mellow Mood*.

Having said all that, let me admit that most church budgets don't have enough funds available to pull off such a coup. As with all other aspects of Youth Ministry, you'll have to make do with a fraction of what your dreams would require.

It can't be any worse than when I was stuck with a portable cassette player and a set of headphones as my only system of music reproduction. Okay, it could have been worse…they could have been ear buds. At least I had the option of cranking it up as high as I could and having everyone sit as close as possible to the headphones. The 2.5 inch speakers didn't make much noise, but they certainly helped the youth group practice togetherness.

The Walls

Decorating the walls of the youth room can either be an exciting creative adventure, or an excursion into the pits of hell itself. Gee…guess which of those two options you'll experience more often.

Sure, there will be the times of communal mural-painting, but there will also be seasons of frustration as teens fail to agree on anything. You'll experience the thrill of creating graphic designs out of the bright hand-prints of group members, but you'll also feel the wrath of preacher's wives who claim jurisdiction over all matters of color and taste(lessness) within the church building.

The most useful tool in decorating the walls of the youth room is a good supply of posters. These can be marketing posters from record companies, inspirational posters like "Jesus Is My Homeboy," or periodic tables from the high school science teacher. The most important thing is that they are available to cover up the holes in the wall from when the elder's kids were playing "Toss the Freshmen."

The Reality

All that I've said so far is meaningless when you stand face-to-face with the reality with which most Youth Ministers are saddled: The teens in your church are not important enough to warrant a space of their own.

Okay…that sounded a little harsh. What I should have said has something in it about stewardship of financial resources and the necessity to share space for multiple functionalities and the congregation's top three goals of zzzzzzzzzzzzzzzzzz….

WE'LL LEAVE THE LIGHT ON FOR YOU

Often, whether in the context of a weekend conference or statewide youth rally or ministering to the elders' children in the regional federal penitentiary, you will have the *opportunity* to stay in a motel with the precious adolescents in your charge.

I say *opportunity* because I'm not accustomed to using the type of terminology that would more realistically describe the experience.

Well…I suppose it's not really all that bad. It's better than a blazing two-by-four up-side the head. I suppose.

* * * * * * *

The joy starts with the delicate balance of finding just the right motel. It can't be expensive: all areas of youth ministry require the utmost diligence to live on the cheap. But it can't be *too* cheap or parents won't feel it is safe enough to allow their kids to go. You'll need to settle somewhere between the Ritz Carlton and Charlie's No-Tell Motel. But if you could find something run by Charlie's less-trashy cousin….

It also needs to be within a reasonable distance to the event involved, which means you need to start early before all the available rooms in the area are gone. Which means you'll actually have to book the place before you know how many teens will be involved. Which means you can't use any of the Save-A-Ton-Of-Money-But-You-Can't-Cancel websites, because your initial estimate of how many rooms you'll need *will* be wrong.

It's not all bad news, though. Take heart, knowing that you will be sleeping in a bed all by yourself, because there's not a teen on the planet who isn't creeped out by the thought of sharing a bed with you. There will always be at least one student who will volunteer to just sleep on the floor, claiming that he or she likes it. In reality, they just want to be closer to the door so they can sneak out when you go to sleep.

Wait a minute…did I inadvertently imply that you would actually be getting any kind of restful sleep during this adventure? Oops…sorry about that, Chief. The truth is, you had better be a light sleeper so your flock doesn't fly the coop. They would like nothing better than to have a story to tell the majority of their friends (who stayed home) about roaming the hallways of the motel or going to a 24-hour oxygen bar while the old-as-dirt youth minister sawed logs.

But all of this is ignoring the overwhelming truth that it won't be until 4:07 AM that the little *darlings* will be quiet enough to approximate the beginning of a semblance of a nap.

* * * * * * *

A tried-and-true tradition of the youth group motel stay is having a pizza delivered to the room. This event is treated with the same excited anticipation as a visit from the President or the release of the new CD by Carpe Tunnel, *Seize the Crawlway*.

It doesn't matter that each and every precious soul under your watchful tutelage has had pizza 87 times a month for the last seven years of their lives. They will still treat the ordering of pizza delivered to the motel room as the highlight of whatever faith-filled extravaganza you happen to be attending: "Dude! You shoulda been there, man! We ordered this *huge* pizza and it took like forever to get there and when it got there the guy had this *huge* zit on his chin! It was so totally gross! And then there wasn't any sausage on the pizza, so we totally got him to give it to us for half price, dude! I mean, dude! You shoulda been there!"

* * * * * * *

The elephant-in-the-room yet to be discussed is the focal point of any fine motor lodge's décor: the television. Monitoring what gets displayed on the one-eyed monster is yet another reason why you won't be getting much sleep. It's bad enough if the little lust-bombs you're sharing a room with sneak a peak at some R-rated movie on HBO, but that is nothing – I repeat, it is *nothing* – compared to the damage likely to be inflicted upon your reputation (if not your actual personal body) if the church treasurer examines the receipt from your motel stay and finds a charge for the viewing of *Snow White and the Seven Full-Grown Men*.

Trust me.

Really.

BUT SERIOUSLY, FOLKS

There's plenty more that can be written about the wild, wonderful, wacky world of being involved in the spiritual upbringing of teenagers in a local church setting…but I'm already losing money on this whole deal, so what's the point?

Well…the point is – and always has been – a person needs a sense of humor to get through it all. My youth ministry professor, Dave Roadcup, told us, "A youth minister without a sense of humor is like a car without a bumper." And it's true: You *are* going to get knocked around a bit, so you need to have some protection.

The good news is, it's almost never as bad as what the chapters in this book would lead you to believe.

Almost never.

The better news is, it's worth it all when those guys who drive you crazy in your discipleship group list you as their hero on their personal web pages.

The best news is, this ain't all there is. There's a goal way down the road that should encourage you to keep pressing on. Come to my party in the northeast corner of heaven, and we'll laugh about our scars.

"Therefore, my dear brothers, stand firm. Let nothing move you. Always give yourselves fully to the work of the Lord, because you know that your labor in the Lord is not in vain." *1 Corinthians 15:58*

CPSIA information can be obtained at www.ICGtesting.com
Printed in the USA
BVOW04s1726180713

326194BV00002B/594/P